TURNING POINTS

OF THE

SPIRIT

A journey from institutional
religion to authentic spirituality

GLENNIS JOHNSTON

Published by Fire-Light Books in 2016
Email: firelightpublishing@gmail.com

© 2016 Glennis I. Johnston

All rights reserved.
No part of this publication may be reproduced
in any manner without prior written permission
of the publisher.

ISBN   9780994639806

Key topics include:
emerging Christianity, progressive theology, the historical Jesus, institutional religion, spirituality, process theology, biblical interpretation, culture and religion

Cover Design by Joanna Holden
Printed in Australia by Ingramspark

ACKNOWLEDGEMENTS

I wish to acknowledge those who have helped me to gather my thoughts into book form. John Bodycomb and Lorraine Parkinson very patiently read my first draft, giving many helpful comments. I am indebted to Patti Tooth for her invaluable proof-reading assistance.

Without the practical and moral support of my husband, Craig Johnston, I would not have had the opportunity to write. Thank you for believing this project was worthwhile. My children, Joanna and Andrew, have encouraged me and provided critical feedback from the perspective of another generation. I am grateful for the invaluable support of my friend on this faith journey, Lesley Bryant, without whose encouragement I might have been too distracted to write.

CONTENTS

1.	Religion With or Without Spirituality	1
2.	A Personal Journey	26
3.	Why Break with Traditional Christianity?	52
4.	The Pros and Cons of Church Ministry	74
5.	The Bible as a Stumbling Block	91
6.	What to Make of Jesus, The Central Character in Christianity?	112
7.	The Dark Side of Institutional Religion	144
8.	The Bad Mix of Culture and Religion	181
	i Colonialism, Racism and Christianity	188
	ii The Earth, Religion and Spirituality	201
	iii Gender Inequality	211
	iv Pluralism, the New Cultural Setting for Religion	215
	v Cultural Identity and Fundamentalism	222
	vi Cultural Values of Success and Growth	226
	Culture and Religion Conclusion	229
9.	Reimagining God	232
10.	Should We Reinvent the Church?	263
11.	A New Paradigm for the Spiritual Life	284
12.	Looking Forward	304
	Recommended Reading	322

PREFACE

Increasingly, Christians are uneasy with inherited doctrines. Progressive ideas confront church-goers with unsettling challenges to core beliefs. Frustration grows when their local churches seem unable to cope with probing questions surrounding the scriptures and the divinity of Jesus. Discontent becomes serious for those who wrestle with the negative institutional tendencies exhibited by religious organisations. More Australians than ever before are questioning the relationship between religion and spirituality.

Genuinely devout people of faith are held to their religious group membership through personal identity and lifelong bonds of loyalty. For those brought up in a religious tradition, following the path to a new faith paradigm can feel both urgent and daunting. Hope and anxiety are par for the course when a faithful Christian dares to explore the issues raised by modern scholarship and new faith perspectives. Some retreat into the comfort of conservative doctrines with renewed zeal. Others enter the confronting and exciting transition phase where there are more questions than answers. Those who seek a more satisfying perception of *God*, the scriptures, faith and spirituality pursue their quest without the support of institutional religious bodies. Fortunately, stories, books, scholarly research, internet forums, pod-casts and conferences provide resources for the journey. Those who have the courage to honestly re-examine the assumed beliefs of a lifetime are heartened to discover they are not alone.

This is the story of a search for spiritual integrity. My quest has led me from the heart of institutional religion into a new faith paradigm. I was steeped in the teaching of the Church, served as an ordained minister, pursued higher studies in New Testament and gave voluntary work in a multi-faith organisation. My development of an alternative faith perspective has been slow, steady and multifaceted. This book is both a reflection on the significant experiences that became turning points on my own journey, as well as an exploration of the issues that confront all people of faith. I hope that these reflections on the interaction between religion and spirituality will encourage others who have set foot on a similar path.

Glennis Johnston
Dorrigo 2016

CHAPTER ONE

Religion With or Without Spirituality

Previous generations of Australians have associated spirituality with religion and with Christianity in particular. Our current generation no longer makes that connection. Religious institutions are facing an image crisis on the outside and on the inside, a clash of beliefs and identity. Progressive Christians are creatively working to reinvent the Church while conservatives are upholding traditional doctrines with renewed devotion. Throughout the world, religious and nationalist fundamentalism is on the rise. Ironically, in this era of advanced education and scientific discoveries, institutional pressure to conform to belief systems is as strong as ever. At the same time, there is a growing and widespread longing for a spiritual life that has integrity in the face of global communal challenges.

First, some clarification of terms. I use the word 'religion' to refer to a belief system associated with specific written texts called scripture, historical traditions and promoted by a structured religious community, be it the

Church[1] or another defined historical organisation. 'Spirituality', as I am using the word, is an on-going experience, set of values and commitment to live in a meaningful and connected way with the world in both its material and unseen sacredness[2].

'Spirituality' is a dirty word amongst many church-goers. And 'religion' has pejorative connotations for some who consider themselves 'spiritual but not religious'. For the sake of understanding, I hope that we can set aside those simplistic and unhelpful assumptions for the duration of this story. When I refer to authentic spirituality I am excluding those pseudo-spiritual practices that are all about me feeling good. My understanding of an authentic spiritual life is one that leads me beyond myself to care for 'the other'. Spiritual experience includes a wide range of encounters with inner impulses such as love, generosity, compassion, forgiveness, creativity, connectedness, and the Life Force that many of us call *God*.

The majority of our contemporaries use the word *God* assuming that others know who or what they mean by that term. I no longer make that assumption, and often prefer to find other words altogether because *God* means different things to different people. Nevertheless, I will

---

[1] I use the term Church with a capital C as a collective term for all Christian organisations that claim to be a part of the Christian Church in some way. With a small c it refers to specific churches, denominations or local expressions of the broader Church.

[2] Places, objects or events that speak to us of a divine presence and beauty are typically described as sacred. I use the word sacredness to imply that this world is filled with such places, creations and experiences that hint of the ever present divine impulse.

occasionally refer to *God*, asking my readers to set aside the common connotations of that word until I explore its meaning in a later chapter.[3] I acknowledge also that many friends have what they describe as spiritual experiences without ever making reference to *God*.

The term 'religion' is often used to refer to anything that smacks of belief in the unseen dimension of life. But for this conversation that use of the word is too broad and will confuse what I wish to share. Therefore, to be on the same page, I will limit use of the word 'religion' to the narrow definition above. Even with this distinction, it is too easy to set one against the other, implying that authentic spirituality is rarely found within the Church or other religious organisations. That is a gross misjudgement of religious adherents. I have known too many wise people of faith within the Church who demonstrate a deeply inspiring spirituality to draw that conclusion.

Globally, religions provide countless human beings with a framework within which they find meaning for their lives. Belief structures allow people to connect their experiences of love, forgiveness and generosity with an image of the ultimate and eternal reality, often named as *God, Allah, Yahweh, Elohim, El Shaddai*, the *Lord of Hosts, Bhagavan, Brahman, The Almighty* and many other names from different traditions. This linking of what human beings intuitively experience as good with a description of the divine, gives meaning and a sense of purpose. Unlike some critics of religion, I do not scoff at religious life when it is humbly and genuinely lived. Although in most

---

[3] I will come back to this central issue in chapter nine, *Reimagining God*.

instances I do not accept the belief structure of their religion, I respect the honourable intentions and the inner life of large numbers of faithful religious adherents.

But human experiences of the divine can be, and need to be, separated from the religious framework to which they are often attached. The reality is that, as much as any other time in history, religious loyalties now create barriers to a harmonious society. It needn't be this way, if only a moderate, humble and inclusive approach to religion was widespread. And yet, despite a well-educated public, we have seen a rise of religious fundamentalism across the globe, including within Christianity.

It is fair to say that for millions of people throughout the centuries, the outward forms of religion have mediated an experience of the sacred. Marcus Borg, a pioneering author in the field of 'emerging Christianity', described this as *the sacramental nature of religion*.[4] He argued for the necessity of the outward forms of religions, including the Christian Church, in providing this sacramental function for humanity. I agree that we all need a community of memory and practice to sustain our spiritual journey. I also respect the positive role of religion in providing a ready framework for humble people to channel their prayers and worship of a transcendent divine Spirit.

However, in this age of broad education, institutional religious frameworks and belief systems need to hold up to the scrutiny of ethical standards and good scholarship. Increasingly, religious adherents are drifting

---

[4] Marcus Borg, *The Heart of Christianity*, p. 213.

away from their religious institutions because they are no longer satisfied with the answers offered by their authorities and traditions. For the sake of this growing section of the community, it is important to stress that the community of memory and spiritual practice does not need to be found within a religious institution.

Before embarking on a rigorous critique of institutional religion, I hope that we can acknowledge the paradox. There have always been individuals who, living and breathing the teaching of the Church, have sought to live lives that are faithful to a loving, holy and generous *God*. They have grown in personal humility, shown compassion towards the suffering, and desired to love their neighbours and at times even their enemies as Jesus did. Not for a moment should we deny the genuine spiritual maturity of such people.

This brings me to a critical premise that I hold in this conversation. It is one of the realities and fundamental concepts that is rarely understood. *Our experience of the numinous[5] or spirituality on the one hand, and our theology or beliefs about God on the other, can be significantly out of step with one another.* This principle is rarely recognised either inside or outside of religious institutions. It is usually assumed that correct religious belief is tied to authentic spiritual experience. My observations of Christians from various traditions and friends within other

---

[5] The term *numinous* was popularised by the German theologian Rudolf Otto in 1917. He described the numinous as evoking an experience of fear and trembling, as well as attraction, fascination and feeling compelled. It has been used by many since to refer to the mysterious, the holy, the divine or the supernatural.

faiths have led me to conclude otherwise.

Let's explore the various dimensions of this premise with a few examples. There have been some outstanding leaders whose lives of service or courage in fighting corruption in the Church or society are legendary, but who nevertheless expressed certain beliefs or attitudes that we would now disavow. Such heroes of the Faith within Christianity have not been porcelain saints. Like all of us, they have at times shown us *God* and at other times left us disappointed. I immediately think of Martin Luther, Augustine of Hippo and more recently, Mother Teresa.[6] No doubt if we had the opportunity to sit at length with any of these remarkable characters we would find we disagreed on a number of significant points. Yet despite the disappointments, I would not for a moment want to cast suspicion upon the valid spiritual experiences of these

---

[6] Martin Luther courageously tackled the excesses of the Roman Catholic Church in the 16th century, leading to major reforms and making the scriptures and faith more accessible to ordinary people. He challenged the financial and spiritual oppression of church members by the Roman Church hierarchy, wresting access to and interpretation of the scriptures from the hands of the clerical authorities. Yet we find ourselves shocked to discover that he also held antisemitic views.

The spiritual conversion of Augustine of Hippo (354 - 430) is legendary. Yet his callous abandonment of his mistress and his teachings on sexuality and sin that steered the Church's idea of piety for centuries is now somewhat of an embarrassment. Further, in his later writings he condoned the use of violence and the torture of heretics in an attempt to convert them to the 'true' Faith.

Mother Teresa (1910 - 1997) was a Catholic nun whose work of compassion with the dying in Calcutta is legendary. Yet we hear stories of the harshness with which she treated her novices.

courageous fathers and mothers in the Faith[7].

This fundamental premise also affirms that the presence and leading of the divine impulse is not limited by the intellectual understanding or beliefs that a person has about *God* and life. The gracious presence of the divine spirit connects with us when our hearts and minds are receptive, despite the many blind-spots in our religious assumptions. We are complex human beings. We may fail to examine our more questionable beliefs such as materialist, sexist or racist attitudes, while still being able to glimpse the love and beauty of *God* in our moments of humility or gratitude. It is commonplace for human beings to have emotional/spiritual experiences of the divine presence without making any thoughtful connection between these experiences and other dimensions of their lives.

In other words, I reject the notion that any of us is either right or wrong, good or bad, in all aspects of our lives. The link between our experiences, our reasoning and our motivations is never simple. All of our religious heroes are a strange mixture of wisdom, love, misguided thinking, shame and brilliant insights. There are shades of grey, darkness and brilliantly lit colours within all our lives. This remains true irrespective of our spiritual experiences or the religious beliefs we hold dear.

Belief systems are rarely thought through. Most of our deeply held beliefs are taught to us as children before we begin critical thinking. By the time we are young adults most of us have put our religious beliefs into the 'corner

---

[7] The Faith (capital F) refers to the traditional Christian belief system.

cupboard' of our brains marked 'religious' - the one that is not allowed to be opened for intellectual scrutiny. It seems that the *God*, whose presence we sense at those rare times of openness or need, does not force us to confront our racism, our ambitions, our inconsistencies. We ourselves have to choose to go there. We ourselves have to decide that we will ask the questions that disturb our comfort and challenge our long-held assumptions. Unless we choose that uncomfortable journey of questioning, most of us live with a bunch of inconsistencies that we try to suppress or explain away.

The development of an examined and consistent spirituality happens only when we make a conscious decision to subject our worldview and beliefs to ruthless scrutiny. Such scrutiny is not undertaken easily. This decision is usually made when we are confronted with new information that we cannot escape or a personal crisis that shakes our equilibrium. Unless experience forces us to re-examine our religious assumptions, it is less disturbing to live with the inconsistences. Is it any wonder the spiritual directors tell us that a personal crisis, defeat or suffering in some way is essential for a healthy spiritual journey?[8]

Our own personal transformation is an ongoing lifelong experience. Fortunately, we don't need to have thought through a mature and consistent belief system before we can have some encounter with the mysterious

---

[8] Spiritual director, Richard Rohr, makes this point regularly in his writing. Religion is largely populated by people afraid of hell; spirituality begins to make sense to those who have been through hell, that is, who have drunk deeply of life's difficulties. (Things Hidden: Scripture as Spirituality. Note in particular pp 62-100.)

and loving divine presence or *God* at the centre of our lives. Even as a teenager, with an inadequate knowledge of the world, and unresolved questions about who or what *God* is, I occasionally experienced a sense of a divine presence that sustains life. Although I realise how much I have learned since my teens and twenties, I do not now disparage the experiential spirituality of my younger self. Despite immaturity, the experiences I had then of a divine presence were a strength to me during those years.

Like us all, my spirituality was related to, but not entirely dependent upon, my belief system. It would be many years later, after significant educational, vocational and personal experiences, before I radically re-examined my religious assumptions. Unfortunately, this honest scrutiny of beliefs, with its accompanying personal growth, does not always happen. I know many compassionate, mature Christians who have never allowed for any development or change in their doctrinal presuppositions. Often this has required them to perform a kind of theological acrobatics in order to fit their experience of life into what they assumed they must believe. These Christians live with a disconnect between their traditional beliefs and their personal values and experiences. Oftentimes, that disconnect is not even recognised because there is simply no critical examination of beliefs at all. And typically, if they do become aware of inconsistencies they are explained away as 'mystery'.

A large proportion of Church members keep their belief system unquestioned in their sacred mental cupboard, and refuse to open it in case the light of day reveals its flaws. They presume that to question the teaching of the Church would amount to being unfaithful to the *God* whom they love. They have never been able to separate their love *of God* from the Church's doctrines *about God*. They presume that to question one is to diminish the other. Typically, they criticise those of us who challenge traditional doctrines as being unfaithful to *God*.

Considering this matrix of motivations and loyalties, I am convinced that there are two slightly different reasons preventing many Christians from embarking on a journey similar to my own. For some, there is that deep fear of being unfaithful. They do not want to question 'truths' that would amount to losing their faith. Secondly, they fear being left with no solid ground of meaning for their life. The reasons people oppose progressive thinking about faith are not merely intellectual. If they were, the discussion would be much easier.

I would like to assure anyone wanting to explore this questing spiritual journey that the first fear is simply not valid. To struggle courageously with questions of belief and meaning is an important component of personal growth. How then can it be an offence to *God*? Is our faithfulness to be directed towards that which we call *God* or towards the set teachings of the Church? Can we distinguish between the two? My invitation to fellow travellers is to undertake this quest for a consistent spirituality seriously and honestly.

This is not a journey of rebellion or arrogance or a petty reaction to negative experiences. Wherever the journey leads, I believe that humble, honest searching for truth and greater understanding is an honourable task in any human life. This quest is based on the desire to live more meaningfully and faithfully to all that is good. The thought that a loving *God* would discourage such a genuine quest is nonsensical. Just as doubt is not the opposite of faith, so rigorous questioning is not the opposite of honouring truth.

The second fear is valid, however, in that entering into a period of deep uncertainty is par for the course in this journey. But it is not the end. One cannot look critically at the beliefs of a lifetime without experiencing a cognitive and spiritual disequilibrium. There naturally will be a period when one feels uncertain about the ground of one's faith, without knowing what will take its place. Without a spiritual mentor during this process, anxiety and fear may send a religious seeker rushing back to the traditional belief system of their comfort zone. But for those who do not close their minds to new possibilities, the uncertainty of transition leads eventually to a more satisfying appreciation of meaning.

There are many facets to the disconnect between beliefs and spiritual integrity. As mentioned, the uninformed beliefs of our immature years do not prevent a legitimate experience of what we might call the divine or sacred presence. It is also true that many Christians experience spiritual and emotional growth despite never questioning their belief system. Further, children and adults without the ability to assess their religious ideas are not locked out of spiritual experiences. Would any of us presume to deny that those with undeveloped intellects are able to receive and give unconditional love, compassion, trust, forgiveness or beauty - all of which belong to the realm of spiritual experience? And yet such friends cannot articulate any belief system, traditional or otherwise.

Taking this point further, I have some Muslim friends whose inner experience of and trust in *God* is genuine. They have inspired me as I have witnessed the expression of their spirituality on a daily basis. And yet, when I discuss religious belief with these friends I find myself less than inspired. One close Muslim friend, whose love and service I admire, explained to me her belief that doing good earns points with *God* that are then processed into rewards in the afterlife. That concept of a reward and punishment style of *God* leaves me quite unimpressed. I am sure that not all Muslims believe this teaching and also that, subconsciously, some Christians have a similar understanding of *God*. I do not intend to comment on Muslim doctrines in general. I simply observe that some of my personal friends, whose religious belief system I find unattractive, nevertheless inspire me with their lives of love, service and compassion. From my perspective, this is another example of the disconnect between intellectual adherence to beliefs and inner spiritual experience.

Whether from a Christian or other faith tradition, a person can have spiritual values and inner beauty that are notably out of step with the religious teachings they assume to be true. It is more than possible to refute many of the doctrines of the Christian Church throughout the centuries, while acknowledging that within that same Church there have been examples of inspired spirituality. We may abhor the excesses of the medieval Church, for instance, and yet be lifted in spirit by the life-story of Francis of Assisi, who belonged to it. We may condemn the institutional responses of the Church to allegations of child abuse in our own generation, while at the same time find ourselves nurtured by the wisdom of the Church's spiritual directors.

We can distinguish between the individual and the organisation. Of course there are Church members whose lifestyle and attitudes demonstrate an attractive spirituality. However, from what I have observed, the institutional Church in its doctrines and use of power does not demonstrate an authentic spirituality.[9] We cannot simply draw a direct line from the lives of inspirational people to their belief system. The fact that we can find humble, wise, loving and compassionate people within the institutional Church (and within other religions) does not prove that their doctrinal system is sound.

Although I draw immense hope, challenge and inspiration from the life and spirituality of Mahatma Gandhi,[10] this does not prove to me that his religious framework of Hinduism is the theology to base my life upon. Or because I am frequently challenged and spiritually fed by the insights and writings of Richard Rohr,[11] I need not embrace his Roman Catholicism and its

---

[9] I will explore the institutional nature of the Church in more depth later in chapter seven, *The Dark Side of the Institutional Religion*.

[10] Mohandas Karamchand Gandhi (1869 - 1948), leader of the Indian independence movement during the British rule of India taught and practiced non-violent civil disobedience as a tool for social change.

[11] Fr Richard Rohr (1943 -) , is a Franciscan priest, author, spiritual director and founder of the Centre for Action and Contemplation in New Mexico.

doctrines as the guide for my spiritual journey. Although I find depth, beauty and wisdom in the poetry of Rumi,[12] it does not automatically follow that Islam will provide a helpful framework for my spiritual growth. And even though we can admire the generous charitable work of many Christian churches, that does not prove the legitimacy of their doctrines.

The fact that the Church can provide admirable care and advocacy for the marginalised is certainly to its credit. This work is often the result of outstanding individuals who sacrifice much to serve the world around them. Unfortunately, this positive contribution by Christians does not negate the reality of the abuse of power by the Church as a whole and the hierarchy of the Church in particular. I have often heard it said that the Church has made a huge difference to the world in caring for the needy and powerless. The establishment of schools, hospitals and other charitable institutions by the Church is a cause for gratitude. However, we need to think clearly and remember the disconnect that often exists between spirituality and belief systems.

I frequently hear Christians quoting the positive history of charitable works by the Church as proof of the validity of the Faith. Although these inspiring stories do exist, unfortunately it is an argument that does not stand up to scrutiny. A more honest and less selective look at history reveals that on balance the Church's impact in the world does not stack up favourably. And often, if truth be

---

[12] Jalaluddin Rumi, the Sufi Muslim poet (1207 - 1273), focused upon mystical spirituality over against legalistic religion.

told, the motivation behind the establishment of schools or charities has been to pave the way for the conversion of the recipients to Christian faith. Especially in mission settings, the motivation behind charity has often been mixed and condescending. What was once considered a positive charitable contribution to society is now judged by later generations as patronising and lacking in transformative social justice.

Nevertheless, we can be grateful that throughout the centuries there have been some remarkable Christians who have advocated for the compassionate care of the poor. It is possible to celebrate their lives and achievements without using them to justify the unexamined adherence to traditional beliefs. It is critical to understand that our experience of the divine impulse and our doctrines about *God* can be significantly out of step with each other.

It is a sheer grace that so many of us have glimpses of the beauty and magnificence of the divine presence. It is perfectly understandable that we interpret any positive spiritual experience we may have as confirming the religious framework within which we live and worship. But that is a mistake. Imagine a church-goer who, in a contemplative frame of mind, walks on the beach, hears the roar of the waves and suddenly feels an inexplicable reassurance of the existence, love and eternal beauty of *God*. That Christian will almost always interpret their inner mystical experience as reassurance that they believe rightly. They will naturally associate their glimpse of the divine impulse with the *God* whom they have learned about within their church. Subconsciously, the thought process goes like this, "If this transcendent but very close *beauty/love/God* is what I have experienced and I am a Christian, then my Christian beliefs must be true." Positive mystical/spiritual experiences are always assumed to confirm one's religion. It is a natural assumption made by people the world over. But it is not thought through.

Once we understand the disconnect between our experience and our theology, we are then freed to go the next step. Our transformative spiritual experiences, although real to us, do not exempt us from the need to re-examine the doctrines and culture of the religious institution in which we have been formed. This is the step on which most religious people have stumbled. It is not a lack of faith to dare to question the teachings of the Church about *God*, scripture and Jesus. It is not sinful, or even spiritually dangerous, to open that sacred 'mental cupboard' to re-examine basic beliefs. In this era of advanced educational achievement, we have a duty to our community to examine religious doctrines with intellectual and academic rigour.

Perhaps it may help those who are nervous of entering this process to realise that the very early Christians also found themselves courageously re-examining the assumptions of their faith. In respect of this point, it doesn't matter whether the book of Acts in the New Testament is read as a stylized description of events or accurate history. A considerable time after the followers of Jesus had their initial post-Easter experiences, they were forced to re-think what they believed about *God* and the world.[13] We are told that these early followers of Jesus had

---

[13] Consider the biblical book of Acts chapters 2 and 3 where the early

Religion With or Without Spirituality

been too narrow in what they had previously believed. Their inadequate beliefs, which they had held as self-evident, did not prevent them from experiencing the transformative effects of the divine encounter at an earlier stage of their spiritual journey. But their interpretation of those experiences did not hold up to later scrutiny. They had to learn to alter their theology to accommodate changing circumstances and new discoveries. Whatever agenda may have motivated the writer of Acts to frame the story this way, we cannot avoid the simple point that experience and theology do not necessarily line up.

If the earliest Christians learned to reassess their religious presuppositions and to alter their theology to fit with new discoveries and experiences, surely we can be daring enough to do likewise. After all, 'faith' is not intended to be a synonym for stubbornly insisting on a set of beliefs that one must never question. Christians need to be reassured that a ruthless questioning of presuppositions can coexist with an authentic spiritual life. With this reassurance, perhaps more Christians will be willing to undertake this important task.

Why would anyone embark on such an unsettling and disturbing quest when life within the Church, or other religious institution, is so comforting and satisfying? The answer for millions of Christians (and dare I say millions of Muslims, Jews, Hindus and many other faith groups also) is that they see no good reason for doing so. The vast

---

church is described as radical, life-changing and empowered by the Spirit and then chapters 10 and 11 where they were forced to review their beliefs. Although not historically accurate, there is a relevant message within the text as we have it that deserves attention.

majority of people within our major religions do not wish to have their comfort zones disturbed. Understandably, the questing ones are a small minority. In fact, even asking the questions that I have asked myself at the beginning of this journey is considered disloyal by some in the Church. Those who listen to new information and probe for better answers do not win themselves any friends within the establishment.

It takes a certain daring of spirit to question those things that have been ingrained in us from childhood, without quite knowing where we will end up. It takes courage to risk losing one's sense of identity by going back to square one and reconsidering the foundational teaching of one's life. My experience is that the early stages of this quest can be threatening and scary. Those who embark on this journey will sometimes feel as though they are not sure of anything anymore. However, if their inner connection with the divine impulse towards beauty and love is an anchor, such courage will lead to freedom and spiritual growth. That is my story, and fortunately I am not alone.

Growing numbers of Australians tell us that they do not belong to a church but practice some form of spirituality. Having been a minister of religion, I have often been critical of such claims. "Where is the oversight?" we clergy would say. "What is there to prevent people going down some strange path of personal indulgence or fantasy, if the doctrinal oversight of the church is dismissed?" Oddly perhaps, I also am suspicious of some personally defined 'spiritualities' that seem self-centred, lack accountability, are disconnected from informed others and have no moral imperatives. And yet, on balance, the history of the Church has shown that oversight all too frequently becomes an unhealthy control, dictating belief and restricting thought. The Church's oversight has not empowered Christians for the adventure of the spiritual journey.

Where then is the balance to be found? How do we develop cohesive beliefs and values free from negative institutional control, while avoiding a self-serving lifestyle under the guise of 'spirituality'? Those of us who value accountability do not want an alternative spirituality that is arrogantly disconnected from good scholarship, community, ancient wisdom and the moral challenges facing humanity. We need a communal perspective that is at the same time accountable, connected and free of negative control. This is the quest to which I refer in this book. This is the quest that I and literally thousands of others from the Christian tradition have embarked upon.

I am presuming that a credible spirituality is connected with the material and social challenges facing real communities around the world. Our inner life and our outer world are intimately woven together, whether or not we appreciate it. The spiritual life takes seriously issues of war, peace-making, the environment, ethical business practices, crippling poverty, cross-cultural relationships and the struggles of indigenous cultures. I cannot accept that any spiritual perspective on life that is only about my personal experience, divorced from these real world issues, is worthy of the quest.

To assume that an individual could legitimately promote an authentic spiritual perspective that is disconnected from all earlier generations and cultures would be arrogant in the extreme. It would be foolish to cut ourselves off from the deepest and life-giving wisdom of the sages through the centuries. Those of us who pursue spiritual integrity don't want to throw the baby out with the bathwater. We just want to be free to discern and name that which is mere bathwater. We are not seeking novelty. We want that which is real, accountable, wise, connected, informed and transformative. Sadly, that freedom of thought is rarely on offer through the churches who, typically, are doctrinally committed.

As communal beings, belonging and listening to the questing community is essential. I am grateful for the knowledge, insights and honest courage of biblical scholars, spiritual directors[14] and secular researchers. That is not to value human knowledge above divine inspiration, as religious reactionaries may claim, but to affirm that real spiritual insights have nothing to fear from the truth, whoever speaks it. We should fear no new discovery from research, be it in astronomy, biology, psychology, sociology or history. All true knowledge cannot be contrary to the authentic experience of human beings. Scientific research is the exciting endeavour to comprehend ourselves and our world more clearly. It can only enhance our understanding of reality.

My own path has taken me from devout traditional Christian faith into a differently defined and satisfying spirituality. I moved through the heart of the Church, giving service in ordained ministry. I have been stretched

---

[14] Spiritual direction is the slightly misleading name given to the task of being a companion with another person on their spiritual journey. The spiritual director listens to and facilitates the inner reflection of another person in their quest to discover their story within *God's* story.

Religion With or Without Spirituality

beyond my comfort zone by scholarship and inter-faith experiences. And finally, I have struggled to make sense of personal encounters with the negative aspects of institutional life. There have been significant milestones or turning points in my growth and thinking. In the following chapters I tell the story of those turning points that I now consider as essential to my journey. Although these critical reflections may arise differently for others, there is an inevitability about them for anyone wanting to pursue spiritual integrity.

If any person begins this quest from the experience of church membership, sooner or later he/she must deal with the issue of how to read the Bible and what we can legitimately know about the historical person, Jesus. Likewise, we need to address some inconsistencies in what we assume about the nature of *God*. Surely it is also long overdue for Christians to consider the relationship between their institutional church and their institutional belief system. I am aware of many efforts being made to reinvent the Church in this generation. Is this the task to which we should be giving our energy?

Finally, we who were raised in the bosom of the dominant Western culture must have the courage to question its values. How has that cultural perspective shaped our understanding of religious life? What has been the two-way relationship between a Western mindset and the doctrines and mission priorities of the Church both past and present? It is not easy for any of us to step back from our own culture and observe its influence on our thinking. And yet, if we wish to gain a more accurate perspective on the life of the Jewish Jesus, we will need to chip away the encrusted Western lens through which most of us look.

Ideas about *God*, Jesus, morality, injustice, culture, power and institutions - each of these diverse matters is spiritual and intimately related to the others. I bring them together in one book as parts of a whole integrated questing process. However, I recognise that it has taken me many years to work through these different dimensions of spirituality. I would not expect anyone who is beginning to ask new questions of their Faith to complete this journey in the time it takes to read one book. If we dare to look afresh at all of these foundational aspects of our religious life, we ourselves may experience transformation in the process of discovering a new paradigm of faith. We need to have courage and patience as the questions arise within us.

Many creative thinkers have tackled these topics, becoming specialists in the fields of biblical scholarship, theology, mission or social change. But it can be too comfortable and convenient to compartmentalise what we know of the Faith. It doesn't help the spiritual quest to keep all these insights in their separate silos. Biblical scholarship should ask questions of theology that in turn must address questions of institutional history which leads us to re-examine the development of culture and mission. As soon as we challenge the foundations of one we must deal with what we have been taught about the other.

A warning sign might be posted at the beginning of this quest. Anyone who dares upon this journey will enter into an unsettling interim period of transition as they leave behind a former paradigm in search of the new. One needs to allow sufficient time to read, consider, process and contemplate the issues at hand. I am able to write about my own journey only now that I have moved through that disturbing no-man's-land stage of transition and into a more satisfying place.

During this process of rethinking my traditional faith, I have chosen to step outside of those religious and para-religious groups that proved unhelpful to this quest. I know now how important it has been to place myself beyond the very present influence of the Church and other faith-based organisations. During the last few years I have discovered a freedom of thought that is rarely encouraged within the confines of a religious environment. When one is placed geographically and professionally within a particular ideological community, there is always a subtle or not-so-subtle pressure to conform to the group's assumptions about life. It is very difficult to step back and critique the worldview of the culture that surrounds us daily. Having now gained a little distance from institutional faith-based groups, I can affirm a spiritual perspective that both challenges and sustains me.

Many others, both published[15] and unpublished, have proposed similar descriptions of this new spirituality. Although still a minority report within the Church, this network of scholars and spiritual seekers is referred to as 'emerging Christianity' or 'progressives'. Although it is sometimes called the 'Emerging Church', that is misleading because there is no church. This movement has no organisation, structure or hierarchy. It is a global network of people who are sharing their scholarly findings and convictions with each other. Their sharing takes place in

---

[15] See, for example, Marcus Borg, *The Emerging Christian Way*.

small groups of friends, sometimes through conferences, often through the internet and recorded public lectures, and through published books and articles. I am inspired by these writers and I am delighted to be part of what is emerging.

This is not a quest that throws out everything that mattered to us without putting anything in its place. After many years of study and being confronted by uncomfortable discoveries, my faith is both changed and deeper than ever. My hope and trust in the goodness of *God* is stronger because of this journey. However, my understanding of who or what *God* is has significantly developed and no longer corresponds to the traditional religious image of the divine. In the following chapters, I will explore all of these matters one by one. Finally, in chapter eleven, *A New Paradigm for the Spiritual Life*, I attempt to give substance to what I now regard as authentic spirituality. This will always feel like an inadequate attempt to describe something that refuses to stop growing.

I am grateful to many others who have written about their own quest with great intelligence and considerable experience. My own conclusions are not significantly different from theirs, but at some point along the way they have become my own deep convictions. Under *Recommended Reading*, I have acknowledged those who have had the most impact upon my own growth. Their works are all worthy of attention. To each of them I say, "Thank you for encouraging me to search more diligently for understanding."

I cannot describe this journey from the perspective

Religion With or Without Spirituality

of a Muslim, Hindu, Jew, Buddhist or any other religious or atheist person. I have no doubt that any of these other starting points will provide a similar adventurous journey for those who seek a cohesive and satisfying spirituality. Critiquing any of our worldwide religious institutions requires honesty and determination. Because our very identity is tied up with our bedrock beliefs, courage is required of anyone from any background to question the presuppositions of their cultural and religious training. Whether or not we are Christians, this endeavour requires us to be counter-cultural and to be resilient in the face of pressure to conform from friends, colleagues and religious authorities. This is the story of my own quest for a life-enhancing and satisfying spirituality.

Questions for Reflection and Discussion

1. *How would you describe the relationship between your spiritual experiences and your belief system? Does one necessarily depend upon the other?*

2. *Would that relationship be different if you had been born into a Hindu, Buddhist, Jewish or Muslim family and culture?*

3. *In what ways does the word 'spirituality' have both positive and negative connotations?*

CHAPTER TWO

A Personal Journey

I recall still the sensation of rolling down a grassy hillside, feeling the earth spinning beneath me, watching the clouds swirling in the blue sky overhead and feeling very much part of the earth itself. That childhood experience of connectedness with a bigger creation, of which I was just a tiny part, has always felt like a glimpse of *God*. My youthful experience led to a deep conviction that this 'bigger thing' was good and it was love and joy, and in it I was safe.

One would be hard-pressed to find a more unlikely beginning for someone who would love to see both Christian faith and society in general radically transformed. I trace the beginnings of my spiritual journey to my childhood days on the family dairy farm in Queensland. Those early memories speak to me about belonging and security.

Even following my father's heart attacks, when we moved to the city of Brisbane, both of my parents worked long hours to provide for the education and security of my brother, sister and myself. Although not 'well-off', we

A Personal Journey

enjoyed a typical middle-class lifestyle in the post-WWII era in Australia. One learned to be frugal, to abhor wastage and as a virtue, to place hard work way up there between godliness and cleanliness. Going to church in the sixties was pretty standard for a much larger proportion of middle-class Australia than it is now. Although I was taken to Sunday School, our family never talked about *God* at home. We were not an overtly pious family.

During my teenage years the church youth group was the hub of my social life. On Saturday nights we enjoyed social outings together and on late Sunday afternoons we met formally for group discussions about faith before attending the evening church service together. Oftentimes following the worship service, we gravitated to the home of a church member for supper. These were marvellous times. We enjoyed good friendships, explored romantic relationships, had lots of fun and searched for deeper meanings in life, all in a relatively safe environment. It may sound strange to younger people now, but these group experiences were enriched by the adults who welcomed us into their homes on Sunday nights. They respected us, didn't try to tell us what to think or do, engaged with us on issues that mattered and helped us to feel that we belonged. It was a valuable experience of a multi-generational faith community.

When I began to spend extra time talking about the Bible and faith with my friends at the church, I suspect my parents began to worry about me. They hadn't intended for me to take it so seriously. They didn't actively discourage my involvement, perhaps because the alternatives associated with 'rock and roll' appeared to be more dangerous. During these years I gained a thirst for the spiritual life. As teenagers from the local church, we met in small groups to pray and discuss the Bible together. My father died when I was sixteen, at the beginning of my final year of high school. Finding comfort in my faith, that year I took on the role of Study Convener for the youth group, preparing and leading the discussion topics for approximately twenty youth at our Sunday evening meeting. The following year I began studying Social Work at the University of Queensland. It was a momentous time.

I cannot remember a time when my relationship with *God* was not hugely important to me. As young Presbyterians, it was important to us not only to be 'right with *God*' in our inner lives, but to believe the right things about *God*. A right relationship with *God* meant salvation, which meant life after death but also a wonderful sense of satisfaction here and now. For Presbyterians, alongside of all this sat the doctrine of predestination.[16] I remember how we struggled to integrate the idea that *God* predestined some to be saved (and therefore some not) with that of an all-loving *God*. In the end we concluded that it was beyond our understanding and that we were not to judge *God*.

With our emphasis upon a personal relationship with *God*, we Presbyterians were critical of those Methodists across the other side of the highway who, we

---

[16] Essentially this doctrine was born from the teaching that even faith is a gift from *God*. Therefore, if we are 'saved by our faith' we had to ask why *God* gave the gift of faith to some and not to others. This led us to the doctrine of predestination - the idea that *God* predestined only some to be given faith and to be saved. Romans chapter 8, verses 28-30 in the New Testament was the text upon which this doctrine was built.

were told, believed in a 'social gospel'. Their 'watered down faith' that put too much emphasis upon social action as opposed to prayer and belief was dangerous. You can imagine that it was an uncomfortable challenge for us in 1977 when the Presbyterian, Methodist and Congregational churches joined to form the Uniting Church in Australia (UCA). It was especially challenging when my own home congregation actually combined to form one parish with those former Methodists across the highway!

Fortunately, we were led by a wise minister who encouraged us to see beyond our narrow perspective and embrace others who expressed their faith differently. Some of the older folk at the church probably found it even more confronting because the changes expected of them disrupted a lifetime of belief and habit. Some of my friends feared compromising their faith if they moved into the UCA. And so they left us and joined the Continuing Presbyterians where they pursued their orthodoxy with zeal. The primary focus of their objections to the new Uniting Church was its proposed view of the Bible. The UCA did not call the Bible the 'Word of *God*' but stated that in the Bible we could "hear" the word of *God*. The hard-liners insisted instead that the Bible itself was literally the infallible Word of *God* for all time.

A few years later, I met one of my Continuing Presbyterian friends in a bookshop. I was astonished at two things during our conversation: how much I had changed since our days together as Presbyterians and how he managed to fit a mention of predestination quite naturally into his first few sentences! I have no idea whether those friends from my early teenage years ever embarked on a similar journey of rigorously re-examining the Faith. One sad aspect of that formal division of the church of my youth is that divided friends lost touch. Nevertheless, I am grateful that I entered the Uniting Church at that stage of my development. It helped me in my search to understand more deeply the grey areas of life and meaning. It allowed me to explore the documents that form the basis of Christian faith using intelligent and critical tools of study. These different ways of approaching and interpreting the Bible remain just as divisive in the Christian community today.

Years later, I became aware of the negative side of the organised Church[17] that led me to examine the interaction of institutions and the human spirit. Nevertheless, I am grateful that at this formative stage of my life it was a positive church community that nurtured my faith and spiritual quest. This was the era of the 'Jesus movement', with a renewal of faith and piety sweeping across the Western world and bringing the renewed energy of the younger generation into the church. Choruses, guitars and the use of drama were added to the repertoire of hymns and sermons in worship. As young people, we felt we were making a difference to an otherwise very traditional church. As children in the 1960's we were taught never to laugh or talk in church. By the time we were late teenagers, 'fellowship' was valued even during worship services. By the late 1970's, laughter at appropriate times in worship was a sign that the church

---

[17] See chapter seven, *The Dark Side of the Institutional Religion*.

was modernising. The church worship experience for most people has altered dramatically within all but the most rigidly formal congregations during the last fifty years. It has moved from a clergy-led spectator event to an interactive personal participation in a communal worship experience.

The 1970's was also the era of church camps when often eighty to a hundred people of all ages from the congregation would go away for weekends together to have fun, develop relationships and learn to explore our faith in new ways. We recognised the need to build community. Despite having rethought my views on traditional Christianity, those years for me are filled with many good memories. Belonging to a faith community was a source of strength and purpose. I can't help but think that all young people would benefit from such an opportunity to explore beliefs in the context of a caring group that offers stability and acceptance.

Yet this revitalising of the church during the seventies, eighties and nineties only affected the style and music of the faith community, not the core message. One thing missing from my home church experience was any suggestion from our elders that it is OK to question the presuppositions of the Church's teaching. Those training in theological college at that time were being exposed to new ideas from theologians such as Paul Tillich[18]. His

---

[18] Paul Tillich (1886 - 1965), a German American, is considered one of the most influential Protestant theologians of the 20th century. ... *Faith as ultimate concern is an act of the total personality. It is the most centered act of the human mind...it participates in the dynamics of personal life* (Tillich, *Dynamics of Faith*, p.5).

existential approach to faith was a remarkable divergence from traditional belief-centred doctrines. At the same time, they wrestled with the controversial 'situational ethics' of John A.T. Robinson[19]. Within the refined halls of theological colleges in mainstream churches around the world, new ground was being turned concerning how to imagine *God* beyond the Church. However, at my local church we remained firmly entrenched in traditional doctrines. In Queensland at least, ordinary church-going Christians of my generation were not exposed to these liberal ideas.

As teenagers, my friends and I were never told that we could inform our faith with knowledge gained through academic scholarship or critical biblical research. Instead, it was ingrained in us that contrary ideas from beyond the core teachings of the Faith would lead us away from *God*. At the same time as those training for ministry were having these significant debates about the nature of *God*, we in the younger generation were being enthused by the 'Jesus movement'. With its emphasis upon personal religious experience, this movement reached us, not so much through our church leaders, but through popular books and cassette tapes (remember that earlier form of recording sound?) distributed by charismatic Christian

---

[19] Robinson's book *Honest to God*, published in 1963, was hugely controversial. It drew much condemnation from traditionalists but was welcomed by liberals. He built upon Tillich's concept of *God*, not 'out there' but the 'ground of our being'. He introduced situational ethics, suggesting that moral codes were not absolute but subject to circumstances.

speakers. Conservative Christian traditions were being promoted in the Western world through media that crossed the boundaries between denominations. This movement was reinforced by the various waves of the charismatic renewal movement in the 1970's, 80's and 90's. The last decades of the 20th century saw a resurgence of personal piety and dealt a blow to the development of liberal Christian thought.

Because of this enthusiastic pietistic approach, many friends and colleagues of my era in the Church are still faithfully holding to orthodoxy as if it were a protection against losing their faith. When my generation later became lay leaders and clergy within the Protestant churches, it ushered in a renewed emphasis on personal piety and upholding the 'true' teachings of the Faith. From my younger perspective, it's as though the Presbyterians had won the theological battle with the Methodists. The social conscience dimension of faith was alive and well in other sections of the Church. But within my own circle during my twenties and thirties, the 'social gospel' was 'out', and the focus on individual religious experience was 'in'.

Thanks to the positive opportunities afforded to the 'baby-boomers' in Australia during the 1970's, I received a free tertiary education. During this time the seeds of my radical questioning were planted. University does nothing for any student, if it doesn't teach her/him how to ask probing questions. A good education is not merely about the gathering of knowledge but about critical thinking and growing the desire to search for 'truth'. During my Social Work studies, I gained a respect for the unbiased research of good scholarship in any field. Truly worthwhile scholarship is a dangerous, creative and freeing thing. If it teaches people to think for themselves, good education can be a subversive tool confronting institutional religion and other powerful forces in society.

While studying at the University of Queensland, I attended on-campus meetings of the Evangelical Union (EU), an association of Christian students. Speakers at the EU encouraged us to put the same energetic study into our faith as we did with our other subjects. However, they also taught us that holding faithfully to the precepts of our faith and remaining actively involved in the Church were the marks of a true Christian. Unfortunately, even in university, most students of law, the sciences and humanities were all unaware that similar standards of research were being used to study the ancient documents of scripture. So when we were encouraged to put the effort of study into our Christian faith, it meant within the framework of accepted theology. It meant learning what the Bible said, not how it was being critiqued by scholars elsewhere. As a young tertiary student in Queensland, I still remained blissfully unaware of the world of biblical scholarship that existed beyond popular Christianity. Amongst my cohort, we all did.

Despite a rather sheltered upbringing, when I entered professional social work in my twenties I encountered first-hand the struggles of the poor, people with disabilities, the marginalised and the abused. I spent my working hours engaging very closely with vulnerable and disadvantaged people. Every day I heard horrific stories of family abuse and witnessed the cross-generational trauma of deprivation and damaged personalities. But clocking off at the end of a shift, I would return home to the other world of husband and church groups. I contributed to the life of my local church through leading Bible studies, choirs and youth groups. The Church remained my secure 'home', while social work stretched me beyond my comfort zone.

Today, having read the works of some of the spiritual directors such as Joan Chittister and Richard Rohr, I understand more about the tasks of being human at the different stages of life. Although I wish I had been introduced to good biblical scholarship in my twenties, I also know that I was attending to those things that were essential for me at that stage: establishing a home, developing skills, enjoying relationships, nesting and raising children. All these things are important in our growth as human beings. Although there was never a lot of money, there were dreams and love and good times. For every purpose there is a season.

Then my little world was expanded far more than I would have imagined during 1979 - 1980 when I spent two years doing training and then voluntary work with a para-religious group known as Moral-Rearmament (MRA), now called Initiatives of Change. I discovered this group through a friend of a friend and was immediately attracted to it as a way of making faith practical. The visionary goal of MRA was to 'remake the world' and what young person isn't keen to do that? After twelve months completing a course in Melbourne and doing fieldwork in other parts of Australia, my husband and I (at this stage we had no children) accepted an invitation to do voluntary work with

MRA programmes in India for six months, Switzerland for six weeks and Britain for four months. Those two years vastly expanded my experience of the world.

As the MRA voluntary team was multi-cultural and multi-faith, my head was thrown into a spin working closely with like-minded Buddhists, Hindus and Muslims. I struggled to accommodate this experience with my traditional evangelical Christianity. I was also confronted with my unacknowledged racism and began to see life in Australia from the perspective of the first peoples of this country. Making friends with indigenous Australians, I learned about their culture face to face. I learned to have a vision for the unique worth and contribution of every person I met. I learned that quiet listening to the inner voice could help me in my decision-making and that there is a moral edge to faith that is transforming. On the practical side of life, I learned the power of hospitality, the combination of genuine care and physical work. These experiences and inner discoveries were all like precious nuggets of spiritual insight that have stayed with me to this day.

MRA /Initiatives of Change aims at bringing change in society through change in individuals. There is a strong conviction that human nature itself is the source of the problems of the world and that if human nature can change there is hope for whole nations. The change I experienced within myself during that time came as I learned to accept responsibility for my own life, relationships and decisions. I have friends who have been inspired by MRA to make some significant life-changing decisions in their relationships and direction in life. These positive

A Personal Journey

experiences remain real, even if they are inadequate in themselves for understanding the complexities confronting our world. Just as with my earlier experiences in the Church, I will always be grateful for the contribution that MRA made to my life experience as a young adult.

Unfortunately, there was no teaching within MRA concerning systemic problems, those global and institutional systems that perpetrate poverty and injustice. We were not trained to critically examine or confront the conservative institutions that supported the status quo at the expense of those who are marginalised. We were taught that the only hope for social change comes from change in influential individuals within social systems. Inspiring stories were told of encounters between people that led to significant change in individuals. Courageous action by those individuals affected broad communal and even international change.[20] Perhaps because these stories have become legendary within MRA, there has been an insistence on seeing this as the only way to bring about change. Advocacy for vulnerable people and open engagement in the discussion of public policies did not get a mention within the ideology of MRA/Initiatives of Change.

Being church-going Christians, the majority of those whom I met within MRA in Australia saw their voluntary work there as an extension of their faith. But

---

[20] Perhaps the most treasured story is that of Irene Laure, socialist member of parliament in France following WWII, whose hatred of the Germans was transformed during a visit to the MRA centre in Switzerland. Following this personal change, she made a remarkable contribution towards healing the rift between the two nations.

despite the involvement of some teammates from other religions being integral to this work, these Christians held on to the traditional faith paradigm. Although many of these friends were 'full-time religious workers', they had no more knowledge than the average church-goer of the scholarly debates surrounding Christian doctrines and scriptures. Unfortunately, with all the goodwill in the world to bring about change for the better, a university education was not encouraged within the MRA team at that time. Spiritual and moral training was valued more highly than a secular education. Fortunately, that set of values has now largely changed.

Through MRA I was taught that faith has a moral backbone and that relationships can be restored through apology, forgiveness and genuine listening to the other person's or group's experiences. Examining the moral dimensions of one's life could be freeing and transformative. But the risk of excesses was high. Any group that focuses so intensely upon outward behaviours is in danger of confusing life-giving insights with stifling moral judgements. Most prominent on the list of moral priorities was absolute honesty and the call to absolute purity. MRA/Initiatives of Change has broadened its understanding of purity in recent decades to include inner motives. Unfortunately, in those earlier years when I was there, it was narrowly applied to relationships, dress and all things connected to sexuality.

Looking back now, I realise that some of the moral tenets of MRA in those days had a lot to do with a fearful attitude to sex. Sexual relationships were believed to be both sinful out of marriage and a lesser choice within

A Personal Journey

marriage. Dating prior to engagement was treated with distrust and not encouraged. For some decades, even marital sexual relationships were regarded as appropriate only when couples had 'guidance from *God*' to have children. In this respect MRA was not unlike some conservative churches of the mid-twentieth century, perhaps with an extra touch of ideological zeal. It should be said that the thinking of the team has changed significantly since that time, as it has in the churches also.

Nevertheless, the stretching experience of working with people of other cultures and faiths was invaluable for a rather sheltered, white, young Australian woman. I learned about the importance of apology and forgiveness in the process of reconciliation between individuals and communities. I was challenged to face the hurts of history, especially in relation to the indigenous people of Australia. I learned how to share my own experiences of growth and always to hold out the possibility of creative change in others from the lowly and humble to the movers and shakers in society. Although there were some negatives, on balance these were two very creative years for me.

Following those two years with MRA, I returned to Queensland in 1981 and took up social work again. This time I worked in Crisis Care, a branch of the state department responsible for child and family welfare. During four years as a shift worker, I was constantly engaged in crisis counselling and child protective work. Almost every day I found myself talking with someone who was suicidal or in trauma from dysfunctional relationships or abuse. Every day for four years I was able to put a human face to crippling poverty and dysfunctional lifestyles. I appreciated being part of a close knit team of professionals and the chance to hone my skills in social intervention. That professional career ended as I moved into a radically different phase of my journey. When I gave birth to my first child, I left the workforce and learned about life from a whole new perspective.

Physically and emotionally demanding, parenting contributed immeasurably to my spiritual journey. Of course having children is not a choice everyone has. But I was fortunate to have that experience of loving a tiny human being totally dependent upon me for life and sustenance. If we allow it to happen, the demands of parenting can teach us what it means to live for someone other than ourselves. More than any other experience in my life, caring for my two beautiful children taught me about self-giving love, especially at those times when I didn't feel I had the energy.

Then, unexpectedly, I came to one of those turning points in my spiritual journey that was filled with amazing discoveries. Radical change was on the way. It didn't happen overnight. The revolution began in 1989 when I entered theological college and began training for the ordained ministry in the Uniting Church. Once I set my foot on that path, my thirst for an authentic and informed life of faith kicked in. It had been twelve years since I had left university with my Social Work degree in hand. Now, with two little children under school age, I was becoming a student again. And I loved it. This time study wasn't about gaining my degree so I could enter the professional workforce. As perhaps it often happens for mature-aged students, study, rethinking and searching for new insights

A Personal Journey

all became incredibly exciting.

Finally, I was in a place where it was OK to ask the questions that I had never been able to ask in a local church setting. I discovered that there is a network of Christians who are processing what we have learned from the biblical and history scholars over the last hundred years. These scholars fearlessly search for an understanding of the biblical documents independent of the dogma of the Church. It was only the beginning of the journey, but it was definitely a beginning. My supportive earlier years in the Church had stood me in good stead for adult life and faith. Now I was moving into the slightly scary, exciting and uncharted territory of biblical scholarship.

Having graduated from theological college in my late thirties I entered parish ministry with many answers, even more questions and still with a fresh enthusiasm for interpreting the scriptures. I enjoyed engaging with church members who had a desire to grow and learn. Aware that I still wanted more answers, I returned to college part-time to extend my knowledge of Koine Greek, the language of the New Testament. At the risk of looking like an eternal student, this enabled me to complete a two-year research Honours Degree at Griffith University in New Testament Studies. Finally, I was able to grapple with some of the issues that had always sat on the periphery of our sights in theological college. I now had the confidence to ask more probing questions of the Church's belief structures.

Life journeys are rarely like highways. More often than not, they are like small country roads whose twists and turns take us by surprise. It was during my forties that an unexpected turning in the road confronted me. On a personal and emotional level, I was taken into a space that I never thought I would enter: that of marriage breakdown and divorce. The grief associated with that loss of a significant, long-term relationship is difficult to describe for anyone who has not been through it. Yet, although I would never have asked for it, I am grateful that through those years of transition, I learned so much about myself. I grew personally in ways that I might not have done otherwise.

During the early days of caring for my school-aged children alone, I was also looking after a reasonably large Uniting Church parish in Queensland. The challenges of leading that congregation through significant change gave focus to my work and definitely helped me through a difficult phase. In fact, the non-judgemental care that members of that congregation showed to me was enormously supportive. I am also grateful that although this phase was naturally difficult for my children, they have matured into delightful and competent adults who still teach me so much. There are some twists and turns in our journey that none of us would choose to map out for ourselves. And yet with hindsight, we often realise how these difficult stretches of the road have contributed significantly to who we've become. I am grateful for all of them.

A couple of years later I remarried and a new chapter of my personal journey began. It seems the story is never finished until it is finished. And, just like the advertisement for steak knives, it's here that I say, "And there's more!" It was during the year of 2008 - 2009, while in parish ministry, that my spiritual quest took off exponentially. Life had brought significant changes. I was remarried, my mother had recently died of cancer and my children were now young adults out of school. My personal life had been full of changes bringing with them grief, newness and hope, all important in themselves. Then, during that particular year, three separate learning experiences propelled me along the path of discovering a new faith paradigm.

The first came from my professional supervisor in ministry, Rev Dr Geoff Prentice, who introduced me to process theology. The more I read and meditated upon these philosophical and theological concepts, the more excited I was to find fresh insights that resonated with my own experience. This theology challenged me to rethink the nature of *God*. It was stretching, disturbing and comforting all at once.

The second turning point came about in 2008 as I attended a national TEAR Australia conference near Sydney where New Testament scholar, Ched Myers, was a keynote speaker. Although Myers' book, *Binding the Strong Man: a political reading of Mark's Gospel*, had been on my shelf for ten years, it was only on hearing him speak that I comprehended the extensive nature of his scholarship. I remember driving home to Queensland after this conference thinking, "Wow! I've got to re-read and rethink so much." I was already convinced that the Western Church had shaped Jesus according to its own image. After engaging with Myers' perspective on the Gospel of Mark, it was no longer possible for me to retreat into a safe and comfortable perspective on the life of the historical Jesus.

The third experience that propelled me on the path to a new faith paradigm was my decision to enrol in a two-year part-time Retreat Leaders' Formation Course. Our course leader was Rev Ross Kingham of *Barnabas Ministries*, based in Canberra. From the moment our small group of students began this journey with Ross, I knew I had come 'home'. Here was the depth of spirituality that would provide me with solid ground upon which to stand as I questioned so much else. The course gave me the tools to tap into the wisdom of the sages, past and present. The practice of contemplation and the insights of various spiritual directors have helped me to develop inner resources of the spirit, avoiding a mere intellectual quest.

So it was, at a particular time of my life, when my parish ministry was stable and rewarding and I was entering perhaps the best years of my career, that I entertained radical new thoughts. Perhaps the sun did not revolve around the earth after all. I began putting together in my head and my heart new understandings of scripture and Jesus, a fresh and non-orthodox concept of *God* and a renewed experience of spirituality that was independent of Church dogma. Each of these aspects of my journey strengthened and enabled the others. All that I was learning in biblical scholarship and theology resonated within my spirit and made sense intellectually. It was not possible to unlearn what I had learned. I had embarked upon a paradigm shift in my world and faith perspective. There was no turning back.

I began to feed some of these new insights into my parish work and always found significant numbers of church-goers who were eager to discover more.

A Personal Journey

Unfortunately, I also found myself within a conservative culture in the church where very few clergy were associated with progressive Christianity. I had heard progressives dismissed and even ridiculed by significant church leaders. Only those who preached orthodoxy were widely respected in the church around me at that time. It was also at this point that I became even more aware of the questionable use of power by the church's hierarchy.[21] Despite good relationships in my local congregation, I realised that I did not wish to simply keep the machinery of the church ticking over. My commitment to the institutional Church would be diminished, unless there was broader support for the re-examination of the doctrinal and cultural assumptions of the institution itself. There was no such support.

Perhaps not surprising then, I retired from ministry and in the beginning of 2011 moved to Melbourne to work with Initiatives of Change. I had hoped that working in a multi-cultural context would provide more freedom to be myself and develop more inclusive ways of approaching faith. It soon became obvious to me that this was not the answer either.

It had been more than thirty years since I first participated in a study course with Initiatives of Change, then MRA. This time I spent three years in Melbourne in order to give voluntary work as the Spiritual Director of a multi-faith live-in community in the Initiatives of Change centre. Having become all too aware of the negative institutional possibilities within the Church, I was looking

---

[21] I reflect upon these experiences in chapter seven, *The Dark Side of Institutional Religion*.

for a community beyond its borders through which to make a positive contribution. And so, when I returned to Melbourne I was hoping to work with a team with more freedom of thought, unfettered by doctrinal conformity and institutional tendencies.

I found it a very strange experience to re-enter a network that had been so meaningful to me over thirty years earlier. I was amazed to find that so little had changed during those years in both the membership and perspective of the team. It was like stepping back in time. Some might value that as consistency and persistence. But I had hoped that the multi-cultural nature of the work would have moved the group beyond the traditional faith paradigm. Surprisingly, at least in its in-house meetings, the group was still using the language and assumptions of old-style traditional Christianity. Paradoxically, it seemed to me that these well-intentioned and dedicated individuals, who had helped me gain such fresh insight in my twenties, were hampered in developing new insights by their own institutional culture.

Perhaps it is an obvious lesson that most of us learn. Rarely can we successfully return to a place of the past. Unless our perspective grows with our community, or it grows with us, we will naturally end up at different places. Despite my respect for many friends there, I recognised that I was out of step with that team's assumptions and expectations. So much had happened in my life and moved in my thinking during those intervening years, that it was not possible to fit back easily into a group that had not moved in the same direction. Although I am grateful to have had those three years in Melbourne, I needed to look elsewhere for a community with whom to explore a new faith paradigm.

Reflecting upon my experience with various faith-based organisations, I noticed a relationship between religious beliefs and religious establishments. I began to ask questions about the connection between formal and informal group dynamics and the nature of indoctrinated group beliefs. I have learned that the desire for conformity and small group power plays can damage the spiritual authenticity of any group in which they take hold. We need to recognise the very influential interplay between individual beliefs and institutional culture.

This struggle to come to terms with the very nature of religious or faith-based institutions has been an integral part of my spiritual quest. For me, this is not simply a matter of social psychology or organisational theory. On the one hand it has to do with the spiritual forces of trust, respect, allowing space for new insights and listening to the voices of those on the fringes. On the other hand, it also stems from observing the opposite forces of personal control, conformity, fear of newness and opposition to criticism. I discovered that orthodoxy does not set people free to seek the divine impulse but attempts to define what that divine impulse must look like for members of the group.

When I was in theological college, I remember a lecturer drawing a circle representing the boundaries of belief. Inside of the circle were the Trinity and the life, death and resurrection of Jesus. We were told that it is possible to have divergent views on a host of matters outside of the circle such as evolution, homosexuality and worship practices. But if we disputed the core beliefs inside the circle, we could no longer call ourselves Christians. At that time, most of us in college felt good about placing ourselves inside the circle. The pressure to conform to the thinking of a group of people, whom we respect and with whom we share our lives, is powerful and multi-layered.

The vexing question for many is whether a group, that outwardly seeks to honour *God*, must be protected above the individual. This is both a philosophical and spiritual dilemma. The reality is that the social and religious groups to which we belong exert an enormous influence over our worldview and our perception of the divine. Irrespective of the group's stated intentions, not all these influences are freeing and nurturing to the spirit. We need to learn to step back from our ideological surroundings and question the practices, values and culture of our group. Of course no group is perfect. Every organisation will have its faults and areas for improvement, just like ourselves. This reality requires us to be patient with each other. But in the end, we each have to decide exactly what we are comfortable working with and weigh up the net effect of the group upon our own spiritual journey.

While weighing up my options concerning working with these various religious organisations, I kept coming back to my conviction about *God*. I believed that *God* is always the one who draws human beings towards transparency, beauty, freedom and love. When any group's culture imposes constraints on what may be talked about, it pushes individuals in a different direction and smothers the experience of the divine impulse. For me, these two -

response to the divine presence and adherence to the expectations of the institution - became incompatible.

That part of my quest was particularly difficult because most of my friends are comfortable working within faith-based institutions in order to make a positive contribution with their lives. I appreciate the good intentions and giftedness of my friends still working faithfully within the networks that I have now left behind. I recognise also that others may be helped through these organisations, as I was at earlier stages of my journey. However, my own experience afforded me a particular insider's/outsider's perspective on those institutional systems. Each of the organisations, that had once been a helpful framework for my personal development, no longer provided me with a path to an authentic spiritual life.

We human beings need community and will always form groups for a multitude of good purposes. Other than for time-limited periods of retreat or reflection, I doubt we can develop authentic spirituality apart from the experience of community. Accordingly, I have struggled with the question of how any group can avoid becoming more important to its members than the individuals with whom it engages. This is not about individualism per se, that lacks the values of community. It is about transparency, ethical conduct and respect for each person, no matter how seemingly insignificant. It is about not elevating any group identity or leadership to a place above scrutiny. This is the challenge for those of us who seek to develop non-institutional communities around the new faith paradigm.

Having accepted that building spiritual community

within an institutional framework or team was not for me, I chose to take another unmarked turn on that country road. I felt the need for a space that allowed for more freedom of thought and expression. And so, at the beginning of 2014 I embarked on this current stage of my journey. Here in rural NSW I enjoy the adventure of writing, engaging in new forms of community, running a B&B and retreat centre and enjoying the beauty of the moment. I am grateful for all the experiences, both uplifting and painful and even the 'mistakes' that have led me here. It is a joy now, not so much to have arrived at some end point, but to have reached a place in my thinking that is both satisfying and coherent with all that I have learned.

I do not intend for this book to be academic. Using as little specialist language as possible, I would like to take the reader on this journey with me. One could leap ahead to chapter eleven to discover where I have landed. But those readers who struggle with some of the questions that I did along the way - the Bible, Jesus, the nature of *God*, institutionalism and culture - may be interested to follow how this search evolved into a whole new perspective on life. In the following chapters, I will explore how each of these critical issues became 'turning points of the spirit' on my journey.

A Personal Journey

Question for Reflection and Discussion

How would you describe your own spiritual journey and the experiences and discoveries that have influenced it?

CHAPTER THREE

Why Break with Traditional Christianity?

It was Saturday night in the seventies. The city was crowded with people streaming into cinemas, couples having romantic restaurant dinners, friends finding ice-cream parlours and buskers entertaining on the pavement. As I approached the corner near Festival Hall, a voice called out, "Are you saved?" He was standing on an upturned metal tub as he pursued his passion to save the souls of passers-by. As a young committed Christian, I might have been keen to reassure him that, yes, I was saved. Instead, cringing inside, I anxiously hoped for the green 'walk' light so I could make my escape.

It seems like a caricature of traditional Christianity. And yet, reduced to its fundamentals, this evangelical stereotype is reasonably faithful to traditional doctrines of what it means to be a Christian. The reason I cringed at the public questioning of my relationship with *God* had more to do with the breaking of social etiquette than our disagreements over the purpose of Jesus' life and death. Mainstream churches may recognise the subtleties

Why Break with Traditional Christianity?

of society, but doctrinally they affirm the same belief system as that soap-box preacher.

Chances are my readers will be familiar with the tenets of traditional Christianity. But for those who are coming at this from another vantage point, the following is a short summary of what the Church has traditionally taught. After clarifying the traditional faith paradigm, we can then consider some of the doctrinal issues whose questioning the Church has resisted. Although there are some doctrines taught in the Roman Catholic Church that the Protestant churches do not espouse, by and large the following beliefs have been common to Christians of all varieties.

The foundational document of Christianity is the Bible. After more than two hundred years of debate within the Church, these particular writings were elevated to the status of the canon of scripture in the late fourth century - although there was some controversy over the canon during the Protestant reformation of the sixteenth century. Some churches, such as the Uniting Church in Australia, do not hold that the Bible is literally and historically accurate in all respects. Nevertheless, most Christians consider the Bible to be the unique 'word of *God*'. Even within the Uniting Church, although many members are happy to read some of the narratives as metaphor, that's as far as they go in taking liberties with the scriptures.

Traditional Christians believe in a *God* who is not just one *God* but a Trinity: "Father, Son and Spirit". The Father, the creator of all, has an eternal love relationship with Jesus *Christ*, the *Son of God*. According to this teaching, the *Son* existed before the creation and became 'incarnate' (made flesh) in the person of Jesus, during the early first century. Following his crucifixion and death, Jesus was bodily raised to life by *God* and later ascended into heaven to be with *God* the Father. We relate to Jesus now as the *Christ* of faith. *Christ* is the Greek word for the Jewish *Messiah*, meaning anointed one. The *Holy Spirit*, another 'person' of the Trinity, is described as *God* being active in the life of the world and individuals. Although the idea of a triune *God* was not developed in the time of Jesus or even when most of the New Testament was written, it became the hallmark of orthodox Christianity. Since the creeds were established in the fourth century, the concept of the Trinity has been the essential core of Christian belief.

Regarding our relationship with *God*, the Church has taught that we human beings are all sinful by nature and that this has life and death consequences. The price to pay for sin is eternal death following the judgement by *God*, that comes either after our own death or at the end of the world. However, according to the tradition, because Jesus lived without sin himself, his death and suffering paid the price for us so that at the judgement we are pardoned and offered eternal life with *God* instead. This doctrine is known as substitutionary atonement, because Jesus' suffering and death has been substituted for our own.

Linked to this idea is an emphasis upon the spilling of blood as part of the sacrifice. It harkens back to the very ancient Jewish belief in forgiveness of sin for the people of Israel, through the shedding of blood. Ceremonially, blood was shed by the killing of a sacrificial lamb at the temple

Why Break with Traditional Christianity?

on the Day of Atonement. Hence, Jesus is often referred to as the 'Lamb of *God'* who died 'for our sins'. There is some confusion in the Church about the source of this tradition, with other suggestions that it refers to the lamb's blood that was painted on the two doorposts and the lintel of the houses of the ancient Israelites at the original Passover. We are told that *God* killed all of the first born sons of Egypt, forcing the hand of Pharaoh to let the Hebrews go. In that story the Hebrew children, on the eve of their escape from slavery, were spared from slaughter by *God* because they were covered by the mark of the lamb's blood. According to a tradition written into the New Testament documents, this deliverance from death was reinterpreted by Jesus at the time of his last supper, to refer to his own blood and death.

Although this language has faded in some mainstream churches, still today in many Christian communities, songs are sung about the 'saving blood of Jesus'. I know Christians who still speak enthusiastically about being 'washed in the blood of the lamb'. When I was ministering on the Gold Coast, I participated in the Emmaus movement. This lay-led movement for the renewal of faith was very strong on traditional doctrines and one of their favourite songs celebrates "the power, power, wonder-working power in the precious blood of the Lamb". This same image is embedded in the most treasured ritual of the Church - the Holy Communion or the Eucharist, in which the wine that is sipped is said to be "the blood of Jesus".

Many of my clergy friends ministering within the

Church are as uncomfortable as I am with this emphasis upon blood. They even rewrite the liturgy surrounding the Holy Communion to avoid this theology. Many of us have questioned the very ancient concept of a judgemental, exacting *God* who requires a blood sacrifice in order to forgive. But the critical thinking of these friends is like an underground movement with no official approval. The fact is, the idea that Jesus' blood was shed to save us from eternal death, is as core to the traditional Christian paradigm as the belief that Jesus was *God* incarnate.

It should be noted that, by tradition, this substitutionary shedding of Jesus' blood does not provide forgiveness for everyone but only for those who consciously accept it. We do this by believing in Jesus and accepting that he is our Saviour. This personal choice is made in prayer, and its consequence of going to heaven rather than hell is what most Christians refer to as 'salvation'. Hence the stereotypical preacher astride the soap-box on the street corner asking passers-by, "Are you saved?" This old-time-religion style of evangelism concentrated entirely upon salvation and the forgiveness of sin. Although the Catholic Church did not adopt the same evangelistic style, Catholicism has also focussed on salvation as life after death. For Catholics, salvation through the death of Jesus was only available within the framework of the Roman Catholic Church itself, and only if symbolised by the ritual of baptism.[22]

---

[22] Because of this belief, generations of Catholics would rush to baptise an ill new-born, afraid that if the child died unbaptised he/she would not go to heaven. The exclusionary beliefs of the Roman Catholic Church